Mona T. Johnson

TURN UP
PRAYER PULL DOWN
STRONGHOLDS

DEVOTIONAL JOURNAL

MONA T. JOHNSON

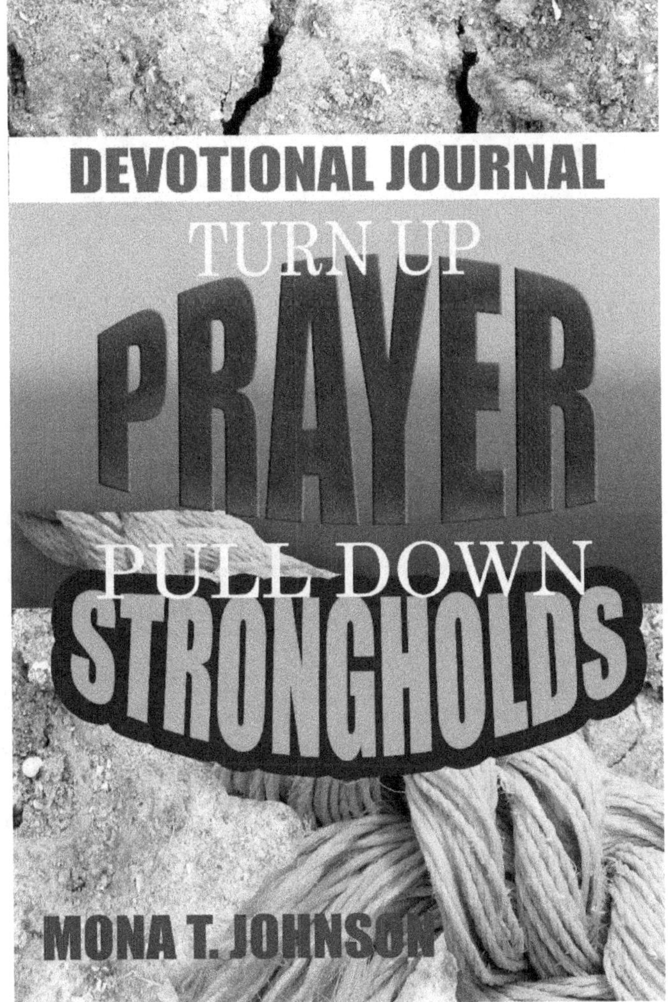

DEVOTIONAL JOURNAL
TURN UP
PRAYER
PULL DOWN
STRONGHOLDS
MONA T. JOHNSON

Turn up Prayer Pull Down Strongholds Devotional Journal
Copyright © 2016
Mona T. Johnson

Published in the United States of America

Library of Congress – Catalogued in Publication Data

ISBN-13: 9798747151628

Published by Jabez Books
www.JabezBooks.com
(A Division of Clark's Consultant Group)

Unless otherwise indicated all scriptural quotations are taken from the King James Version of the Bible.

DEDICATION

This book is dedicated to the two loves of my life; my inspiration, my second born child, Lorenzo, my intercessor, who constantly prayed for me year after year, and stood with me through every trial and tribulation imaginable and my third born, Arielle, my angel, my armorbearer who was sent to me by God. I love you both.

Table of Contents

INTRODUCTION

Just as Jesus prayed for the young boy with demons to be set free, Elijah prayed that the rain would stop for three years, and Joshua prayed for the sun to stand still for a day, we, too, as God's intercessors, have the same authority as they did because of the Holy Spirit residing in us. They were mere men such as us, who laid down their lives to serve the Mighty Creator. Definitely, as Christians, we can do mighty exploits for our Father. God created the world in seven days by the words He spoke from His mouth and we can also make our world a much better place through the power of prayer.

In this devotional, you will be provided with prayer scriptures from the Word of God (Holy Bible) to teach you how to have a more powerful, consistent prayer. Praying the Word of God and having faith in God and His Word always gets positive results. We must believe that prayer has the power and authority to change circumstances and conditions, as well as transform lives in our sphere of influence.

This devotional will allow you to hear the very heartbeat of God. It will strengthen, equip and empower you to develop a stronger prayer life annihilating the works of darkness with the *"dunamis" (Greek)* power of the Holy Spirit working through you, in the name and blood of Jesus Christ.

It is time to TURN UP the temperature of your PRAYER and PULL DOWN the STRONGHOLDS of the enemy!!

Chapter 1

WHAT IS PRAYER?

Prayer is communication between God and man. It is a time to come before the Lord to confess, repent, listen, commune and intercede. Prayer is a vehicle by which we can acquire God's will and purposes for our lives and for His people. Through prayer, we can have an intimate relationship with our Father, God. *Psalm 116* states it best, *"Because God has inclined His ear unto me, therefore, I will call upon the Lord as long as I live."*

Available to each born again believer are the sevenfold gifts of the Spirit of God as listed in **Isaiah 11:1-2,** *which are the spirit of the LORD, the spirit of wisdom and understanding, the spirit of counsel and might, the spirit of knowledge and of the fear of the LORD.*

The gifts of the Holy Spirit in **1 Corinthians 12:8-10,** *are the word of wisdom, word of knowledge, gifts of healing, working of miracles, faith, prophecy, discerning of spirits, diverse kinds of tongues, and interpretation of tongues.* The fruit of the Holy Spirit listed in **Galatians 5:22** *is love, joy, peace, longsuffering, gentleness, goodness, faith, meekness, and temperance.*

Jesus says (in the Word of God) if we abide in Him and His Word abides in us, we shall ask what we will, and it shall be done unto us (John 15:7). If we live in Him and His Word lives in us, we not only want what He wants, but we become the means through which He gets it.

Matthew 12:43 states when the unclean spirits leave he walks around in dry places seeking a new home, but when it does not find one, it comes back to its old one, which is your body. If the Word of God is residing in our temples, the unclean spirits will not be able to reside. God's desire is for our temples to house His Spirit. Right now ask God to fill you with the fruit of His Spirit according to Galatians 5:22, Isaiah 11:1-2 and I Corinthians 12:8-1.

Chapter 2

WHY SHOULD WE PRAY?

n prayer, we don't want to spend time asking God for little things. His desire is to do great and mighty things through us. Ask Him for the impossible things. *Look at the prayer of Jabez, it is short, but very powerful. "Jabez cried out to the God of Israel, "Oh, that you would bless me and enlarge my territory! Let your hand be with me, and keep me from harm so that I will be free from pain, (1 Chronicles 4:10 NIV).* And God granted his request.

We should pray because:

It brings God near to us. *What other nation is so great as to have their gods near them the way the* LORD *our God is near us whenever we pray to Him* (Deuteronomy 4:7)? It brings Him closer to us, as stated in *James 4:8 -- if we come near to God, He will come near to us.*

Jeremiah 29:11-12, God says the plans He has for us are to prosper us, give us hope and a great future. As we call on Him, in prayer, He will hear us.

As we hide under the shadow of the wings of the Most High, Psalms 91:1

No weapon formed against us shall prosper, Isaiah 54:17; therefore, we can go boldly before the throne of grace in times of need. Hebrews 4:16.

It commands God's attention; God wants us to. II Chronicles 7:14-15 *says "If my people who are called by my name will humble themselves and pray, seek my face, turn from their wicked ways, then I will hear from heaven and heal the land."*

In Hebrews 11:6, God says He will reward those that diligently seek Him.

God will reveal secret things to us, reveal the mystery of His Kingdom and His will. Then was the secret revealed unto Daniel in a night vision. Daniel 2:19

Unto you is given to know the mystery of the kingdom of God. Mark 4:11

Having made know unto us the mystery of His will, according to His good pleasure which he has purposed in Himself. Ephesians 1:9.

Take some time to read a powerful prayer of repentance in *Daniel, 9th* chapter. God wants us to ask for things that are secret and hidden.

It defeats darkness. *Howbeit this kind goeth not out but by prayer and fasting. Matthew 17:21; Mark 9:29*

And God has raised us up together, and made us sit together in heavenly places in Christ Jesus. Ephesians 2:6.

It fulfills God's will here on earth. *Psalm 115:16, "The heaven, even the heavens are the Lord's, but the earth has He given to the children of men."*

God has given us the keys to the kingdom of heaven and whatever we bind on earth is bound in heaven and whatever is loosed on earth is loosed from heaven. Matthew 16:19

Jesus, the Son of the Living God was in constant prayer with the Father. And it came to pass in those days, that He went out into a mountain to pray, and continued all night in prayer to God. (Luke 6:12)

Then cometh Jesus with them unto a place called Gethsemane, and saith unto the disciples, Sit ye here, while I go and pray yonder. Matthew 26:36

Then was Jesus led up of the Spirit into the wilderness to be tempted of the devil where he fasted forty days. Matthew 4:1-2

Chapter 3

THE POWER OF PRAYER

The reason why prayer is so powerful is because God's Word is powerful. If God says it, we can take it to the bank. Faith, obedience and patience are three keys to powerful prayers.

Faith in God - Look at the promise God made to Abraham. And the Lord appeared unto Abram, and said Unto thy seed will I give this land and there built he an altar unto the Lord, who appeared unto Him. **Genesis 12:7**

For all the land which thou seest, to thee will I give it, and to thy seed forever. And I will make thy seed as the dust of the earth: so that if a man can number the dust of the earth, then shall thy seed also be numbered. **Genesis, 13:15-16).**

When you trust God 100%, you can (be assured) that whatever requests you bring to God in prayer, as long as it aligns with His they will, will be answered. **I John 5:14.**

Take a look at **Hebrews 11**; the faith chapter. When we trust and have faith in God, we rest in Him. If you remember in the Bible the children of Israel could not enter the Promised Land because of unbelief, so they wandered for forty years.

(I Kings 17, James 5:17-18). Elijah prayed no rain would fall for three years.

Joshua 10:12-13 The mighty warrior, Joshua, who in the battle of Gibeon, commanded the sun and moon to stand still for a day and they did. Talk about *powerful prayer, these are examples of mortal men, just like you, saying powerful prayers.*

Jesus said, we shall lay hands on the sick that they shall recover according to **Mark 16:1***; it is not us healing, but God using us as vehicles to get His healing to someone.*

Obedience is the second component of powerful prayers. Deuteronomy 28:1-14

Joshua 1:7 He told Joshua to do all His word commands so his way would be prosperous.

Moses went to Pharaoh and asked him to release God's people even after God told Moses He would harden the heart of Pharaoh. Exodus 5-10

Look at how many times Elijah told Elisha to go and look for the rain clouds. I Kings 18:41-43

Obedience is better than sacrifice. I Samuel 15:22

Patience is the last component of powerful prayers. We can't rush God. Know this, that the trying of your faith worketh patience. But let patience have her perfect work, that you may be perfect and entire wanting nothing. James 1:3-4

And not only so, but we glory in tribulations also; know that tribulation works patience; and patience, experience and experience, hope. Romans 5:3-4

And beside this, giving all diligence, add to your faith virtue; and to virtue knowledge; and to knowledge temperance, and to temperance patience, and to patience godliness. 2 Peter1:5-6

For you have need of patience, that, after ye have done the will of God, ye might receive the promise. Hebrews 10:36

Remember, when we pray, we are praying to an eternal God.

God's Word will accomplish all it was sent to do and will not return void. Isaiah 55:11 states, *"So shall my word be that goes forth out of my mouth: it shall not return to me void, but it shall accomplish that which I please, and it shall prosper in the thing whereto I sent it."*

As we enter into prayer, there will be demonic forces trying to stop us or our prayers from reaching the throne room. This is not the time to back up or become fearful. God has not given us a spirit of fear, but one of love, power and a sound mind (2 Timothy 1:7).

Chapter 4

NAMES OF GOD

We are doing ourselves an injustice when we don't know God for who He really is. To know God's name is to enjoy a kind of privileged access to Him. The definition of "name" is a word or a combination of words by which a person, place, or thing, a body or class, or any object of thought is designated, called, or known.

What's in a name? In Matthew 1:21-23, *"She shall give birth to a son, and you are to give Him the name Jesus because He will save His people from their sins. All this took place to fulfill what the Lord had said through the prophet, Isaiah: "The virgin will be with child and give birth to a son, and they will call Him Immanuel, which means, "God with us." We* see here that "Jesus" means Savior *and*

"Immanuel" means God with us. Many times throughout the Bible, God will name children or even change a name as in the case of Abraham, Sarah and Jacob (Genesis 17:5-6; Genesis 17:15-16; John 1:42; Luke 1:13).

You can see that names are important to God. The names of God provide clues into His divine character.

ELOHIM (e-lo-HEEM) - God, Mighty Creator. *(Genesis 1:1).* As our Creator, He has infinite resources to accomplish His purposes *(Isaiah 40:28-29; Isaiah 41:10; Genesis 28:15).*

EL ROI (El raw-EE) - The God Who Sees Me. *(Genesis 16:13-14).* He always hears our cries. He will never leave or forsake us *(Psalm 33:13-15;*

Psalm 121:3, 5-8; Matthew 6:3-4; Deuteronomy 12:28; Matthew 5:8).

EL SHADDAY (El shad-DAI) - God Almighty. The God who is strong and unchanging *(Psalm 91:1-2, 14).*

EL OLAM (el o-LAM) - *The Everlasting God/The Eternal God (Genesis 21:32-33).* The name for the God who has no beginning or ending. *(Revelation 1).* God's love and faithfulness endures forever. *Isaiah 40:28-31 and 46:4*

YAHWEH (yah WEH) - *Lord.* When we pray to Yahweh, we are praying to a God that draws near to us to deliver us from living a life full of sin; *(Exodus 3:12-15; 20:12-3; Psalm 103; Numbers 6:24-26).*

YAHWEH NISSI *(yah-WEH nis-SEE) - The Lord my Banner.* a God who is able to overcome our enemies *(Exodus 17:15-16). (Romans 8:31).* God has not given us a spirit of fear, but one of power, love, and a sound mind *(II Timothy 1:7).*

Esh Oklah, El Kanna *(AISH o-KLAH, EL kan-NAH)* - Consuming Fire, Jealous God. God is a consuming fire that destroys everything that is opposed to His holiness *(Deuteronomy 4:23-24; Hebrews 12:28-29) (Zechariah 2:5).* He is also a jealous God who wants us to give of ourselves wholeheartedly to Him, and not to worship other gods *(Exodus 34:10-14).*

Qedosh Yisrael *(ke-DOSH yis-ra-AIL)* - Holy One of Israel. Qedosh Yisrael is calling His people to become holy as He is *(Leviticus 19:1-2).*

God says to be Holy, for He is Holy (Leviticus 11:45.

We are made in His likeness and image.
Read Isaiah 6:1-7 and Leviticus 19.

Whatever name we call upon, we have to believe in our heart and have faith that God is the One to whom we can look to for everything. He is the only One who could help us in all situations. He is the One to call upon when we are in trouble. He is the One who can heal every place it hurts. He is the One we can trust and know He will never fail us. He is the One who loves us unconditionally. God's love is a love that gives until it has no need to give more, a sacrificial love (agape).

Chapter 5

HOW TO ESTABLISH A PERSISTENT PRAYER LIFE

Payer is just not asking God for things, it sometimes involves warfare, declarations and decrees, thanksgiving, or sometimes prophetic prayers.

Prayer is communication with God and He wants us to pray without ceasing I Thessalonians 5:17. How can we obtain a persistent prayer life?

- **Develop a personal relationship with God.** Constant communication with God is vital.

The Sovereign Lord has given me a well-instructed tongue, to know the word that sustains the weary. He awakens me morning by morning, wakens my ear to listen like one being instructed. The Sovereign Lord has opened my ears; I have not been rebellious, I have not turned away. Isaiah 50:4-5

And hath raised us up together, and made us sit together in heavenly places in Christ Jesus. Ephesus 2:6

- **Examine the condition of our hearts**. *(Psalm 51)*.

- **Pray according to the Word of God.**
The Lord said to me, "You have seen correctly, for I am watching to see that my word is fulfilled. Jeremiah 1:12

In the beginning was the Word and the Word was with God and the Word was God. John 1:1

The Word of God is sharp, quick, powerful, and sharper than any two edged sword, piercing even to the dividing asunder of soul and spirit, discerner of thoughts and intents of the heart. Hebrews 4:12

- **Pray in faith believing.**

For without faith it is impossible to please God, for those that come to Him must first believe that He is and that He is a rewarder of those that diligently seek Him. Hebrews 11:6

This is the confidence we have in approaching God: that if we ask anything according to His will, He hears us – whatever we ask – we know that we have what we asked of Him.
I John 5:14-15

What is impossible with man is possible with God. Luke 18:27

For no word from God will ever fail. (Luke 1:37

Faith is the substance of things hoped for, the evidence of things not seen. Hebrews 11:1

- **Persevere.** *Persistent, carry on, keep going in spite of difficulties, obstacles or discouragement, continuing in a thing until the end; endurance.*

So Joshua fought the Amalekites as Moses had ordered, and Moses, Aaron and Hur went to the top of the hill. As long as Moses held up his hands, the Israelites were winning, but whenever he lowered his hands, the Amalekites were winning. Exodus 17:10-11

Ask God to strengthen your foundation in intercession for yourself, your family, your church, your city, your state and even your country.

Chapter 6

HOW TO ENTER INTO THE PRESENCE OF GOD

We need to always be in a state of preparedness for prayer. God looks at our hearts, not our works. Psalm Chapters 1-70 and *Leviticus 16 will allow you to worship God at another level.*

We must come into His presence with the right spirit *(read Matthew 5)* in order to offer Him effective prayers as His royal priests and ambassadors.

But you are a chosen people, a royal priesthood, a holy nation, God's special possession, that you may declare the praises of Him who called you out of darkness into His wonderful light. I Peter 2:9.

When Jesus Christ died, the veil was ripped in half and now we have access to enter the throne of God with boldness where we can obtain grace and mercy in a time of need. Hebrews 4:16

How do we prepare our hearts and minds to enter God's presence?

- *Appropriate God's grace:*
  (Deuteronomy 28)
  Ephesians 6:17

- *Put on Righteousness:*
  Romans 6:18
  Ephesians 6:14

- *Put on truth and honest.*
  John 6:13
  Ephesians 6:14

- <u>*Cleanse ourselves with the Word*</u>:

  (Ephesians 5:25-27).

  Isaiah1:16

- <u>*Worship and Praise God*</u>:

  John 4:23-4

  Ephesians 6:13

- <u>*Separate yourself*</u>:

  John 17:17-19

  Joshua 7:13

  Ephesians 6:15

- <u>*Believe*</u>:

  Hebrews 11:6)

  Luke 1:37

  I John 5:14

  Ephesians 6:16

- <u>*Give God the glory:*</u>

  Isaiah 42:8; 48:11).

- <u>*Wash in the Word:*</u>

  Deuteronomy 1:11i

  Ephesians 6:17

- <u>*Remain in the anointing.*</u>

  Ephesians 6:18

  James 4:8

Set a date with God and keep it and make sure you are on time.

Chapter 7

THE MODEL PRAYER/KEYS TO ANSWERED PRAYER

How are you doing so far? Let's take a look at the Lord's Prayer in *Matthew 6:9-13* in greater detail. Jesus used this model to teach His disciples how to pray. This prayer is God-centered, exciting, creative, productive, scriptural, strategic, practical, transformational, intimate and relational.

Section I – Intimate Praise & Worship – Our Father, who are in Heaven. Hallowed be thy name – verse 9.

Acknowledge God as our Father, our Creator. Offer Him thanksgiving for things He has done or will do in our lives.

Enter into His gates with thanksgiving and his courts with praise. Psalm 100:4

".... but in every situation, by prayer and supplication, with thanksgiving present your requests to God." Philippians 4:6

Section II – Praying God's Will - Thy kingdom come, thy will be done on earth as it is in heaven — verse 10.

We should begin our conversation asking God what is His will for mankind. Ask Him what it is He wants to talk about? What's on His mind? What is it that He wants to pray about through me today? When we do this, God will write His tablets on our hearts.

Section III – Praying Your Needs - give us this day, our daily bread—verse 11.

But my God shall supply all your need according to His riches and glory by Christ Jesus. Phillipians 4:19

Can you trust God to provide for you today?

Section IV – Praying for Forgiveness – forgive our debts, as we forgive our debtors—verse 12.
In whom we have redemption through the blood, the forgiveness of sins according to the riches of the grace. Ephesians 1:7

God says we are to forgive your brother's sins seventy times seven in one day. Matthew 18:21
Section V – Praying for Protection – Lead us not into temptation, but deliver us from evil--verse 13.

There hath no temptation taken you but such as is common to man: but God is faithful, who will not suffer you to be tempted above that ye are able; but will with the temptation also make a way to escape, that ye may be able to bear it. I Corinthians 10:13

VI – Kingdom Praise & Worship – For thine is the kingdom and the power and the glory, Amen-- Verse 13.

Psalm 135

For the Lord is a great God and a great King above all gods. In His hands are the deep places of the earth, the strength of the hills is His also. The sea is His, and he made it: and His hands formed the dry land. Psalm 95:3-5

Let's not forget one very important key in prayer, which the model prayer doesn't address and that is **FAITH**.

As stated in Mark 11:23, we can move mountains with it. In Matthew 17:20 and Luke 17:6 all you need is faith the size of a mustard seed (looks like the size of a pencil lead), and let's not forget Hebrews 11:6 says, for without faith it is impossible to please God.

Faith is the substance of things hoped for and the evidence of things unseen. Hebrews 11:1

There are three important keys related to faith: 1. Faith is supported and sustained by the Word of God. 2. Faith always obeys the Word of God, and 3. Faith trusts God

These all died in faith, not having received the promises, but having seen them afar off, and were persuaded of them, embraced them, and confessed that they were strangers and pilgrims on the earth. Hebrews 11:13

Faith comes by hearing and hearing the Word of God. Romans 10:17

Chapter 8

HINDRANCES TO PRAYER

Although we know when we come to God in prayer, asking earnestly in faith, our requests will be answered. Sometimes, during prayer, it might not seem as though things are moving, believe me, God's angels are always working as long as we are praying the Word of God. There are things that can hinder our prayers from reaching the Throne Room beside demonic forces. We can hinder the fulfillment of God's promises from manifesting. How is that you ask?

<u>Discouragement</u> *–The thief cometh, not but for to steal, and to kill, and to destroy. John 10:10*

Be sober, be vigilant; because your adversary the devil, as a roaring lion, walked about, seeking whom he may devour. I Peter 5:8

Behold, I give unto you power to tread on serpents and scorpions, and over all the power of the enemy: and nothing shall by any means hurt you. Luke 10:19

<u>Sin</u> –*Isaiah 59:2, Psalm 66:18 and I John 2:1 assures us that when we sin, we have Jesus Christ speaking to the Father for our defense.*

For the flesh lust against the Spirit, and the Spirit against the flesh: and these are contrary one to the other: so that ye cannot do the things that ye would. Galatians 5:16-17

Ask God to fill you and give you a fresh anointing with the fruit of His Spirit, which is love, joy, peace, longsuffering, faith, gentleness, goodness, meekness and temperance. Galatians 5:22

Blessed is the man that endureth temptation: for when he is tried, he shall receive the crown of life, which the Lord hath promised to them that love him. Let no man say when he is tempted, say I am tempted of God: for God cannot be tempted with evil, neither tempteth He any man: But every man is tempted, when he is drawn away of his own lust, and enticed. Then when lust hath conceived, it bringeth forth sin: and sin, when it is finished, bringeth forth death. James 1:12-15,

Fear *–There is no fear in love; love drives out fear. John 4:18*

Fear is worry without profit. We are to have faith in God and His Word. God is not a fearful God, and because we are made into His image and likeness, we can boldly call those things that are not as though they were. Genesis 1:26-27, Romans 4:17

Guilt – Guilt is related to the fear of not being forgiven. Therefore there is no condemnation for those who are in Christ Jesus because through Him the law of the Spirit of life set us free from the law of sin and death. Romans 8:1-2

Feelings of inferiority --. We were chosen in Christ long before the earth was made. Ephesians, Chapter 1

We are a chosen nation, a royal priesthood, a holy nation, a people belonging to God (I Peter 2:9).

The foolishness of God is wiser than man's wisdom, and the weakness of God is stronger than man's strength. I Corinthians 1:25

Think of what you were doing in your life when you were called by God. Not many of us were wise by human standards, not many were influential, and not many were of noble birth. But God chose the foolish things of the world to shame the wise. God chose the weak things of the world to shame the strong. He chose the lowly things of this world and the despised things--and the things that are not--to nullify the things that are. I Corinthians 1:26-27. Amen!!!

<u>Doubt</u> *— Ask God for wisdom, He will give it generously. But if you ask, you must believe, not doubting, because he who doubts is like a wave,* *blown and tossed by the wind. That man should not think he will receive anything from the Lord. A double-minded man is unstable in all his ways. James 1:5-8*

God says we shall decree a thing and it shall be established unto us. Job 22:28

We are to call those things that are not as though they were. Romans 4:17

Remember, the children of God could not enter into the Promised Land because of their unbelief.

<u>Wrong motives</u> – *When you ask, you do not receive because you ask amiss, with wrong motives, that you may spend what you get on your pleasures. James 4:3*

Are you asking God to fulfill His Word so you can advance His kingdom?

Bitterness – *If I regard iniquity in my heart, the Lord will not hear me. Psalm 66:8* God hates iniquity, which is a secret sin because we can't see it.

Let all bitterness, and wrath, and anger, and clamour, and evil speaking, be put away from you, with all malice. Ephesians 4:31

Unforgiveness – Then came Peter to him, and said, Lord, how oft shall my brother sin against me, and I forgive him? til seven times? Jesus saith *unto him, I say not unto thee, until seven times: but, until seventy times seven. Matthew 18:21-22*

And when ye stand praying, forgive, if ye have ought against any: that your Father also which is in heaven may forgive you your trespasses. But if ye do not forgive, neither will your Father which is in heaven forgive your trespasses. Mark 11:25-56

<u>Broken relationships</u> - Therefore if thou bring thy gift to the altar, and there rememberest that thy brother hath ought against thee; Leave there thy gift before the altar, and go thy way; first be reconciled to thy brother, and then come and offer thy gift. Mark 5:23-24.

Husbands to be considerate to wives, treat them with respect as the weaker partner and co-heirs so that your prayers may not be hindered. I Peter 3:7.

We are to live at peace with everyone. So let us throw aside anything that easily besets us. Hebrews 12:1.

Chapter 9

PRAYER, SOAKING & FASTING

The definition of soaking is - to lie in and become saturated or permeated with water or some other liquid. That liquid is the Holy Spirit and the Word of God. Soaking is laying in the presence of God until you hear an answer to any question, receive directions, refreshing, healing or that next million dollar idea. He will give you strategic prayer points to pray during your time of intercession.

Try artists like Laura Rhinehart, Pablo Perez, Grace Williams, Roberto & Kimberly Rivera, Ursula T. Wright, Rick Pino, just to name a few. All available on Spotify, itunes, Pandora and of course YouTube and www.soaking.net.

Soaking is more about you becoming one with God. *If ye abide in me, and my words abide in you, ye shall ask what ye will, and it shall be done unto you. John 15:17*

The definition of **fasting** is abstaining from food or drink for a period of time for a spiritual purpose. Fasting is way of obtaining a deeper, intimate, relationship with God.

Is not this the fast that I have chosen? to loose the bands of wickedness, to undo the heavy burdens, and to let the oppressed go free, and that ye break every yoke? Isaiah 58:6

Draw nigh to God, and he will **draw** nigh to you. *Cleanse your hands, ye sinners; and purify your hearts, ye double minded. James 4:8*

Moreover when ye fast, be not, as the hypocrites, of a sad countenance: for they disfigure their faces, that they may appear unto men to fast. Verily I say unto you, they have their reward. But thou, when thou fastest, anoint thine head, and wash thy face; That thou appear not unto men to fast, but unto thy Father which is in secret: and thy Father, which seeth in secret, shall reward thee openly. Matthew 5:16-18

Different Fasts (seek counsel of doctor before starting)

Absolute - because of the extremity of this type of fast, it should be done for short period of times. The absolute fast entails __no__ water or food intake Esther 4:16; Ezra 10:6

Normal - going without food of any kind for a number of days. Drink plenty of water. You may also drink apple juice or broths for your strength Matthew 4; Luke 4:2

Partial - giving up particular foods or drinks for a partial or an extended amount of time. Eating only vegetables, or fasting from 6a - 6p. Daniel 1; Daniel 10

Chapter 10

DIFFERENT TYPES OF PRAYER

Declarations and Decrees

This type of prayer releases apostolic, prophetic decrees. Declarations and decrees are statements of authority. *You shall decree a thing and it shall be established. Job 22:28*

So they established a decree to make proclamation throughout all Israel, from Beersheba even to Dan, that they should come to keep the passover unto the LORD God of Israel at Jerusalem: for they had not done it of a long time in such sort as it was written. II Chronicles 30:5

Then Darius the king made a decree, and search was made in the house of the rolls, where the treasures were laid up in Babylon. In the first year of Cyrus the king made a decree concerning the house of God at Jerusalem, Let the house be builded, the place where they offered sacrifices, and let the foundations thereof be strongly laid; the height thereof threescore cubits, and the breadth thereof threescore cubits. Ezra 6:1, 3

And as they went through the cities, they delivered them the decrees for to keep, that were ordained of the apostles and elders which were at Jerusalem. And so were the churches established in the faith, and increased in number daily. Acts 16:4-5).

Petitions/Supplications

Usually these prayers are asking for favor, mercy, a benefit, wants or needs (spiritually and physically.

Then Esther the queen answered and said, If I have found favour in thy sight, O king, and if it please the king, let my life be given me at my petition, and my people at my request. Esther 7:3

For this child I prayed; and the LORD hath given me my petition which I asked of him. I Samuel 1:27

And if we know that he hear us, whatsoever we ask, we know that we have the petitions that we desired of him. I John 5:15

Supplication prayers pray God's perfect will to be established in a person's life. Most petitions and supplications are made of your own behalf.

Hear, O LORD, when I cry with my voice: have mercy also upon me, and answer me. Psalm 27:7; Psalm 35

Travailing Prayer

Most travailing prayers are birthing prayers; you are pushing things in the spirit.

Before she travailed, she brought forth; before her pain came, she was delivered of a man child. Who hath heard such a thing? who hath seen such things? Shall the earth be made to bring forth in one day? or shall a nation be born at once? for as soon as Zion travailed, she brought forth her children. Isaiah 66:7-8

Then cometh Jesus with them unto a place called Gethsemane, and saith unto the disciples, Sit ye here, while I go and pray yonder. And he took with him Peter and the two sons of Zebedee, and began to be sorrowful and very heavy. Then saith he unto them, My soul is exceeding sorrowful, even unto death: tarry ye here, and watch with me. And he went a little further, and fell on his face, and prayed, saying, O my Father, if it be possible, let this cup pass from me: nevertheless not as I will, but as thou wilt. And he cometh unto the disciples, and findeth them asleep, and saith unto Peter, What, could ye not watch with me one hour? Watch and pray, that ye enter not into temptation: the spirit indeed is willing, but the flesh is weak. Matthew 26:36-41).

Prophetic Prayer

You call those things that are not as though they were. Romans 4:17

And Jesus said unto them, Because of your unbelief: for verily I say unto you, If ye have faith as a grain of mustard seed, ye shall say unto this mountain, Remove hence to yonder place; and it shall remove; and nothing shall be impossible unto you Matthew 17:20.

Prayers of Praise

These prayers are letting God know who He is in your life. *The book of Psalm is filled with adoration of God. (Exodus 15)*

Thanksgiving

Thanksgivings prayers are giving thanks to God for everything in your life. Rejoice always, pray continually, give thanks in all circumstances; for this is God's will for you in Christ Jesus. I Thessalonians 5:16-18

My brethren, count it all joy when ye fall into divers temptations; Knowing this, that the trying of your faith worketh patience. But let patience have her perfect work, that ye may be perfect and entire, wanting nothing. James 1:2-4

Repentance

Repentance is a turning of the heart; seeing the error of our ways, and making a conscious effort to not repeat the same mistake. *Nehemiah 1, Daniel 9*

Then said Jesus, Father, forgive them; for they know not what they do. And they parted his raiment, and cast lots. Luke 23:34).

Warfare

These prayers are literally coming "toe to toe" with the gates of hell.

For though we walk in the flesh, we do not war after the flesh: (For the weapons of our warfare are not carnal, but mighty through God to the pulling down of strong holds;) Casting down imaginations, and every high thing that exalteth itself against the knowledge of God, and bringing into captivity every thought to the obedience of Christ. II Corinthians 10:4-5

You have been given authority over the enemy and nothing shall harm you. Luke 10:19; Psalm 18

But ye are a chosen generation, a royal priesthood, an holy nation, a peculiar people; that ye should shew forth the praises of him who hath called you out of darkness into his marvelous light; I Peter 2:9 who has been given diplomatic immunity. The diplomats (intercessors) —who formally represent the sovereign (God) — is granted certain privileges and immunities to insure they may effectively carry out their duties.

Chapter 11

CHARACTERISTICS & LIFESTYLE OF AN INTERCESSOR

I exhort therefore, that, first of all, supplications, prayers, intercessions, and giving of thanks, be made for all men; For kings, and for all that are in authority; that we may lead a quiet and peaceable life in all godliness and honesty. For this is good and acceptable in the sight of God our Saviour. *I Timothy 2:1-8*

Intercession requires one to have a heart of a servant. But made himself of no reputation, and took upon him the form of a servant, and was made in the likeness of men. Philippians 2:7

And whosoever will be chief among you, let him be your servant: Even as the Son of man came not to be ministered unto, but to minister, and to give his life a ransom for many. Matthew 20:27-28 What about David when he was fighting and was thirsty, his men risked their lives to go across the battlefield, breaking through a host of Philistines to bring back a glass of water. II Samuel 23:15

Ask yourself what can God say about you? Do you have a heart to serve others? Are you being accountable for your actions? Confess your sins, one to another, so that you may pray for each other that you may be healed. James 5:16

Does your life reflect that of one who is sold out for Christ? One that will do anything it takes to live for Christ? One that is willing to let go of the past to live for the future? One who is willing to be obedient to the voice of God? Submit yourselves therefore to God. Resist the devil and he will flee. James 4:7

There hath no temptation taken you but such as is common to man: but God is faithful, who will not suffer you to be tempted above that ye are able; but will with the temptation also make a way to escape, that ye may be able to bear it.
I Corinthians 10:13

But above all things, my brethren, swear not, neither by heaven, neither by the earth, neither by any other oath: but let your yea be yea; and your nay, nay; lest ye fall into condemnation. James 5:12

And there came a leper to him, beseeching him, and kneeling down to him, and saying unto him, If thou wilt, thou canst make me clean. And Jesus, moved with compassion, put forth his hand, and touched him, and saith unto him, I will; be thou clean. Mark 1:40-41

A new commandment I give unto you, That ye love one another; as I have loved you, that ye also love one another. John 13:34

Let us therefore come boldly unto the throne of grace that we may obtain mercy, and find grace to help in time of need. Hebrews 4:16

And I sought for a man among them that should make up the hedge, and stand in the gap before me for the land, that I should not destroy it: but I found none. Ezekiel 22:30

Whatever you bind on earth, is bound in heaven and whatever you release on earth is released from heaven. Matthew 16:19 God has given us those keys to the kingdom of heaven.

But we all, with open face beholding as in a glass the glory of the Lord, are changed into the same image from glory to glory, even as by the Spirit of the Lord. II Corinthians 3:18

Likewise the Spirit also helps our infirmities: for we know not what we should pray for as we ought: but the Spirit itself makes intercession for us with groanings which cannot be uttered. Romans 8:26

Watch and pray, that ye enter not into temptation: the spirit indeed is willing, but the flesh is weak. Matthew 26:41

Howbeit when he, the Spirit of truth, is come, he will guide you into all truth: for he shall not speak of himself; but whatsoever he shall hear, that shall he speak: and he will shew you things to come. John 16:13

So shall my word be that goeth forth out of my mouth: it shall not return unto me void, but it shall accomplish that which I please, and it shall prosper in the thing whereto I sent it. Isaiah 55:11

Behold, I give unto you power to tread on serpents and scorpions, and over all the power of the enemy: and nothing shall by any means hurt you. Luke 10:19

And these signs shall follow them that believe; In my name shall they cast out devils; they shall speak with new tongues; They shall take up serpents; and if they drink any deadly thing, it shall not hurt them;

they shall lay hands on the sick, and they shall recover. Mark 16:17-18

The effectual fervent prayer of a righteous man avails much. James 5:16

Praying always with all prayer and supplication in the Spirit, and watching thereunto with all perseverance and supplication for all saints; Ephesians 6:8

You are the rock that God has built His church upon and the gates of hell cannot prevail against you. Matthew 16:19

The Lord God hath given me the tongue of the learned, that I should know how to speak a word in season to him that is weary: he wakeneth morning by morning, he wakeneth mine ear to hear as the learned. The Lord God hath opened mine ear, and I was not rebellious, neither turned away back. Isaiah 50:4-5.

And hath raised us up together, and made us sit together in heavenly places in Christ Jesus. Ephesians 2:6

Chapter 12

INTERCESSORY PRAYER

This is it! You've made it. I am so proud of you. Congratulate yourself because it takes commitment and persistence to finish anything; two characteristics of God's intercessors. In this Chapter we are looking at what intercessory prayer is and how to use this type of prayer to change your community, your family, the nation and the world. Put your seat belts on and let's go!!

And God said, Let us make man in our image, after our likeness: and let them have dominion over the fish of the sea, and over the fowl of the air, and over the cattle, and over all the earth, and over every creeping thing that creepeth upon the earth. Genesis 1:26

And God blessed them, and God said unto them, Be fruitful, and multiply, and replenish the earth, and subdue it: and have dominion over the fish of the sea, and over the fowl of the air, and over every living thing that moveth upon the earth. Genesis 1:28

If my people, which are called by my name, shall humble themselves, and pray, and seek my face, and turn from their wicked ways; then will I hear from heaven, and will forgive their sin, and will heal their land. II Chronicles 7:14

Prayer, fasting and worship is the threefold cord needed to obtain victory in this realm. When we enter into intercession, we get out of our soulish realm and enter into the spiritual realm.

Thou therefore, my son, be strong in the grace that is in Christ Jesus. And the things that thou hast heard of me among many witnesses, the same commit thou to faithful men, who shall be able to teach others also. Thou therefore endure hardness, as a good soldier of Jesus Christ. No man that warreth entangleth himself with the affairs of this life; that he may please him who hath chosen him to be a soldier. II Timothy 2:1-4

Wherefore take unto you the whole armour of God, that ye may be able to withstand in the evil day, and having done all, to stand. Stand therefore, having your loins girt about with truth, and having on the breastplate of righteousness; And your feet shod with the preparation of the gospel of peace; Above all, taking the shield of faith, wherewith ye shall be able to quench all the fiery darts of the wicked. And take the helmet of salvation, and the sword of the Spirit, which is the word of God: Praying always with all prayer and supplication in the Spirit, and watching thereunto with all perseverance and supplication for all saints. Ephesians 6:13-18

And let us not be weary in well doing: for in due season we shall reap, if we faint not. Galatians 6:9

But ye, brethren, be not weary in well doing. Thessalonians 3:13

And be renewed in the spirit of your mind; Ephesians 4:23

"God says Son of man, the house of Israel (church) is to me become dross; all they are brass, and tin, and iron, and lead in the midst of the furnace; they are even the dross of silver. Ezekiel 22:18

And I sought for a man among them, that should make up the hedge, and stand in the gap before me for the land, that I should not destroy it: but I found none. Ezekiel 22:30

Son of man I have made thee a watchman unto the House of Israel. Therefore hear the word at my mouth and give them warning from me. Ezekiel 3:17

Thy watchmen shall lift up the voice; with the voice together shall they sing: for they shall see eye to eye, when the Lord shall bring again Zion. Isaiah 52:8

For thus hath the Lord said unto me, Go, set a watchman, let him declare what he seeth.
Isaiah 21:6

In Ezekiel 3 & 33, the watchmen warned the people of God's judgment. We are God's watchmen! We are God's gatekeepers! We are God's intercessors!

And when he had taken the book, the four beasts and four and twenty elders fell down before the Lamb, having every one of them harps, and golden vials full of odours, which are the prayers of saints. Revelation 5:8

Watch and pray that ye enter not into temptation: the spirit indeed is willing, but the flesh is weak. Matthew 26:41

Mark 1:3, it says to watch and pray that we will be counted worthy and not succumb to temptation.

Likewise the Spirit also helpeth our infirmities: for we know not what we should pray for as we ought:

but the Spirit itself maketh intercession for us with groanings which cannot be uttered.
Romans 8:26

My sheep hear my voice, and I know them, and they follow me. John 10:27.

And I will give unto thee the keys of the kingdom of heaven: and whatsoever thou shalt bind on earth shall be bound in heaven: and whatsoever thou shalt loose on earth shall be loosed in heaven. Matthew 16:19

As the dew of Hermon, and as the dew that descended upon the mountains of Zion: for there the Lord commanded the blessing, even life for evermore. Psalm 133:3

Who is he that condemneth? It is Christ that died, yea rather, that is risen again, who is even at the right hand of God, who also maketh intercession for us. Romans 8:34.

In the last days perilous times shall come. For men shall be lovers of their own selves, covetous, boasters, proud, blasphemers, disobedient to parents, unthankful, unholy, without natural affection, trucebreakers, false accusers, incontinent, fierce, despisers of those that are good, traitors, heady, high-minded, lovers of pleasures more than lovers of God; having a form of godliness, but denying the power thereof: from such turn away. II Timothy 3:2

For we wrestle not against flesh and blood, but against principalities, against powers, against the rulers of the darkness of this world, against spiritual wickedness in high places so we have to use spiritual weapons. Ephesians 6:12

For by Him all things were created, that are in heaven, and that are in earth, visible and invisible, whether they be thrones, dominions, or principalities, or powers; all things were created by Him and for Him. Colossians 1:16

We must know our weapons of warfare are not carnal but mighty through God for pulling down those strongholds bringing every thought under the obedience of Jesus Christ.

(For the weapons of our warfare are not carnal, but mighty through God to the pulling down of strongholds;) Casting down imaginations, and every

high thing that exalteth itself against the knowledge of God, and bringing into captivity every thought to the obedience of Christ.
II Corinthians 10:4-5

Again I say unto you, That if two of you shall agree on earth as touching anything that they shall ask, it shall be done for them of my Father which is in heaven. Mathew 18:19

It's time to rise up and take our rightful places so that God can restore order, peace, righteousness, and healing. *It's time to call those things that are not as though they were. Romans 4:17*

We have to be faithful, persistent and committed to pray. Either we are going to be a victim or a victor. The choice is yours, which one will you choose?

The heaven, even the heavens, are the Lord's: but the earth hath he given to the children of men. Psalm 115:16

Ye are of God, little children, and have overcome them: because greater is he that is in you, than he that is in the world. I John 4:4

The Spirit of the Lord is upon me because he has anointed me to preach the gospel to the poor. He has sent me to heal the brokenhearted, to preach deliverance to the captives, recovering of sight to the blind to set at liberty them that are bruised. Luke 4:18

Breathe! Are you ready to take back our cities, states, nations, and the world? Are you ready to use the keys God has given you? Are you ready to use the authority that Jesus left with you? Are you ready to take territory for the Lord? Are you ready to do damage in the spirit world? Are you ready to make the devil shudder when your feet hit your floor in the morning? If you answered yes to any of these questions, let go. IT'S TIME TO TURN UP PRAYER AND PULL DOWN STRONGHOLDS!!

AFTERWORD

Congratulations! Man or Woman of God, you've made it to the end. I hope your spirit man and prayer life has gone to another level. I pray that the passion to get into God's presence has become stronger. As you give yourself to God in prayer, praying in faith, He will take care of your every need. I pray God has revealed to you in depth your purpose and destiny for why He has created you. We all have been called as intercessors to stand in the gap for our brothers and sisters until we all come into unity in the faith and the knowledge of our dear brother Jesus Christ. I pray that you have accepted the call and said yes to God and His will for your life. If you want to know how to develop a more intimate relationship with God, check out my other book *"Grace Under Fire"* a prayer/devotional journal that will take you step by step in deliverance from strongholds and reconnecting and renewing your relationship with God.

See you on the battlefield. Grace and peace unto you,

Your Sister in Christ, Mona

ABOUT THE AUTHOR

Mona Johnson was born and raised in Chicago, IL and relocated to Tulsa, OK in 2002. The middle child and middle girl of seven children she is the proud parent of two children, Arielle and Lorenzo; two

 reasons why she does what she does. At an early age of 8 she accepted Jesus Christ and was baptized in the name of the Father, Son and the Holy Ghost. Mona rededicated her life to Christ at the age of 40. This was the point in her life that she truly understood the relationship that anyone can have with Jesus Christ.

Mona was licensed as an evangelist in 2004 and as a minister in 2011 and received intercessory training

under well-known men and women of God in Tulsa, OK. Although she has worked in various positions in the church, Mona feels there is nothing more rewarding and fulfilling than serving God's people, in the area of evangelism and prayer. Mona's passion for intercessory prayer was the driving force behind the birth of Thee Upper Room Prayer ministry because she knows prayer is the only way God's will, purpose and destiny for His people will be established on earth.

Mona is a co-author of Grace Under Fire Prayer/Devotional Journal, 2014 featured author at Jabez Books Reader's Choice Awards; faculty member at the Anointed for Business Leadership Institute in Dallas, TX, Chancellor Dr. Shirley Clark; and Prayer Leader with God's Butterflies Ministry and 90 Day Financial Empowerment Challenge.

Mona is truly honored and humbled that God would use her in the movement of uniting, training, empowering and equipping disciples in the area of prayer in the advancement of His Kingdom.

For speaking engagements contact author at:

P.O. Box 690924

Tulsa, OK 74169

www.theeupperroom.org

REFERENCE MATERIALS

Webster Dictionary

King James Bible

Suzette Caldwell, *Prayers to Change your Life*

Myles Munroe, *Understanding the Purpose and Power of Prayer*

Anne Spangler, *Praying the Names of God*

Brenda Todd, Gap Standers - *Intercession, The Weapon of Choice*

Cindy Trimm, *The Art of Warfare*

Dr. Shirley Clark, *40 Truths About the Ministry of Intercession*

Chi Chi Bismark, *2014 Prayer Summit*

There is a war going on for the souls on this earth and satan is trying to take as many souls to hell as he possibly can, but we have already won the battle. Jesus gave us all power and authority to defeat the enemy and strategies to use as we pull our brothers and sisters from the strongholds of the enemy. Our weapons of warfare are not carnal (flesh), but they are mighty through God to pull down those strongholds. This book will teach you how to stand toe to toe with the enemy, through prayer, using the sword of the spirit, which is the word of God. You will learn what weapons are available to you and how to use those weapons as you engage in spiritual warfare. The most important key to winning a battle is knowing which weapon to use.

As you glide through the pages of this book, you will be equipped and empowered to persevere in prayer winning those souls for the kingdom of God. Not only will you be victorious in winning souls, you will be able to create your ideal world, just by the words you pray over yourself and family members. Jesus Christ died that we would have abundant life and now is the time to live. It's time to turn up the temperature of your prayers and pull down the strongholds of the enemy.

Other Resource Tools By

Mona T. Johnson